Edited by Milton Okun

Associate Music Editor - Dan Fox
Art Director - Gil Gjersvik

ISBN 0-89524-077-7

Old Folks has been omitted because of copyright restrictions.

Performance Suggestions

This folio, based on Kenny Rogers' latest album, is new country music at its best. This is country music that has absorbed many different influences from the pop world as well as the traditional Nashville sounds. Both *She's A Mystery* and *Santiago Midnight Moonlight* have a reggae tinge and should be played lightly with an even 8th note feel. Quarter notes are usually played staccato (short) and the beat must be kept steady in the left hand.

The disco flavor has touched three of the songs, *Tulsa Turnaround, You Turn The Light On,* and *In And Out Of Your Heart* (with its telegraph key introduction reminiscent of the Motown sound of the '60s). The basic idea in this type of music is the double-time feeling in the right hand contrasted with the steady four or eight in the left. Again, the feeling is even 8th notes.

The rest of the songs are more traditionally country, and therefore should be played with the swing characteristic of that style. That is, 8th notes are played rather like ♩3♪ . *Goodbye Marie* has a bright two feeling, but notice the anticipated 3rd beat in the 1st, 3rd, 5th, 7th and many other measures of the song. This anticipated beat must be accented for a proper effect. Although dealing with the time-honored country theme of adultery, *One Man's Woman* has as much pop influence as country as shown by its double-time rhythms and modern chords.

The two pretty ballads in the album are *I Want To Make You Smile* and *You Decorated My Life.* Both make extensive use of modern harmony, chords with alternate bass notes, pedal points, inversions, and suspensions, a far cry from the three-chord songs of yesterday's country stars.

The arrangements reflect Kenny's vocal style as much as is possible on paper. Notice the many grace notes, notes engraved in a smaller size than usual, in the vocal line. These represent Kenny's vocal embellishments, and need not be played on keyboard.

Guitarists will be pleased that every chord diagram has been stamped in by hand. This allows us to suggest logical sequences of chords. Also, in cases where the piano is in an awkward key for guitar, appropriate directions are given for placing the capo. This allows the guitarist to play in a good key while the piano plays in the recorded key. See for example, *I Want To Make You Smile.* This song is recorded in the key of Bb; O.K. for piano but awkward for guitar. So, the guitarist places a capo across the 1st fret and plays in A; guitar then sounds in the recorded key of Bb along with the piano, but fingers in the much easier and better sounding key of A. Of course, if the guitarist doesn't want to play with the record or with the piano, he need not capo as shown.

We feel that this book will please Kenny Rogers fans and lovers of the new country music; the arrangements are well within the reach of the average singer, pianist, and/or guitarist, yet are complete enough for a full sounding, professional performance.

You Turn The Light On

Words and Music by
Stephen Geyer and Lewis Anderson

since you gave me the love I need. You turn the
Guitar → A D D/E A D D/E A D
(Capo up 1 fret)
Piano → B♭ E♭ E♭/F B♭ E♭ E♭/F B♭ E♭
light on, You turn the light on
normal 8va
E7 A A/G D/F♯ Dm/F
F7 B♭ B♭/A♭ E♭/G E♭m/G♭
You turn the light on oo yeah,
A/E E7 A
B♭/F F7 B♭
To Coda
N.C.
dark - ness is gone since you turned the light on.
8va bassa

(N.C.)
Peo - ple who knew_ me___
when I was lone - ly
say they see_ such a change_
(8va bassa till chorus)

___ in me.___
Oo ___ ba - by,
tell them I'm on - ly

D.S. al Coda
guilt - y of love___ in the first___ de - gree. You turn the

Coda
A
B♭
turned the light on.
A
B♭
C♯m
Bm
A
4fr.
Dm
Cm
B♭
C♯m
Bm
A
4fr.
Dm
Cm
B♭

A
A7
D/A
A
B♭
B♭7
E♭/B♭
B♭
E7
A
A
D
D/E
A
D
D/E
F7
B♭
B♭
E♭
E♭/F
B♭
E♭
E♭/F
You turn the light on, You turn the
A
D
E7
A
A/G
B♭
E♭
F7
B♭
B♭/A♭
light on You turn the light on

D/F♯
Dm/F
A/E
E7
A
E♭/G
E♭m/G♭
B♭/F
F7
B♭
Oo yeah, darkness is gone since you turned the light on.
A
A/G
D/F♯
Dm/F
A/E
B♭
B♭/A♭
E♭/G
E♭m/G♭
B♭/F
(You turn the light on, you're turn-in' it on)
Dark-ness is gone since you
A
B♭
turned the light on.
(B♭ 8va)
C♯m
Bm
A
4fr.
Dm
Cm
B♭
(oo - oo oo)
(oo - oo oo)

You Decorated My Life

Words and Music by
Bob Morrison and Debbie Hupp

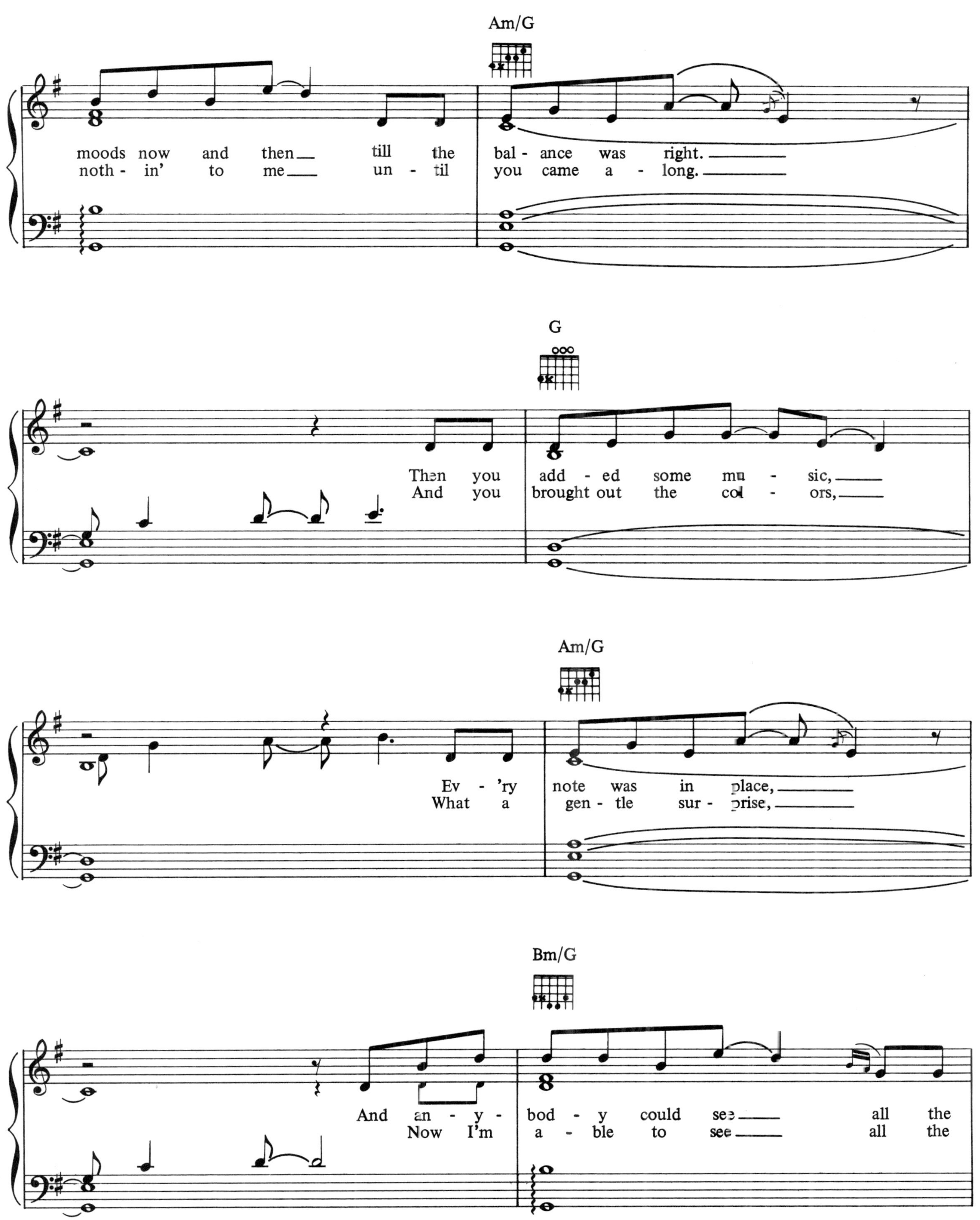
Am/G
moods now and then till the bal - ance was right.
noth - in' to me un - til you came a - long.
G
Then you add - ed some mu - sic,
And you brought out the col - ors,
Am/G
Ev - 'ry note was in place,
What a gen - tle sur - prise,
Bm/G
And an - y - bod - y could see all the
Now I'm a - ble to see all the

Am/G
changes in me by the look on my face.
things life can be shinin' soft in your eyes.
D
G
Gmaj9
And you
f
C
C/D
G
decorated my life,
C
B7
Em
created a world

Em/D
Am7
where dreams are a part.
D
G
Gmaj9
And
you
C
C/D
G
dec - o - rat - ed my
life
C
B7
Em
by paint - ing your
love

Em/D
Am7
all o - ver my heart;
D
G
You dec - o - rat - ed my
life.
B7
1.
C
2. Like a
2.
C
Gmaj7
Slower

She's A Mystery

Words and Music by
Larry Keith and Steve Pippin

F♯m
Bm
told me that I could eas - i - ly fly. But
told me that I could eas - i - ly fly. Well,
Em7
Em7/A
A7
here I am be - liev - ing, And I don't know why.
here I am be - liev - ing, And I don't know why.
D^X
A^IX/D
G^VII/D
D^V
A^V/D
C^III/D
G^III/D
D
10fr.
9fr.
7fr.
5fr.
5fr.
5fr.
Bm
Em7
A7sus4
A7
She's still a mys - ter - y to me, Oh, but she's all I'm

* Instrumental omitted

Goodbye Marie

Words and Music by
Dennis Linde and Mel McDaniel

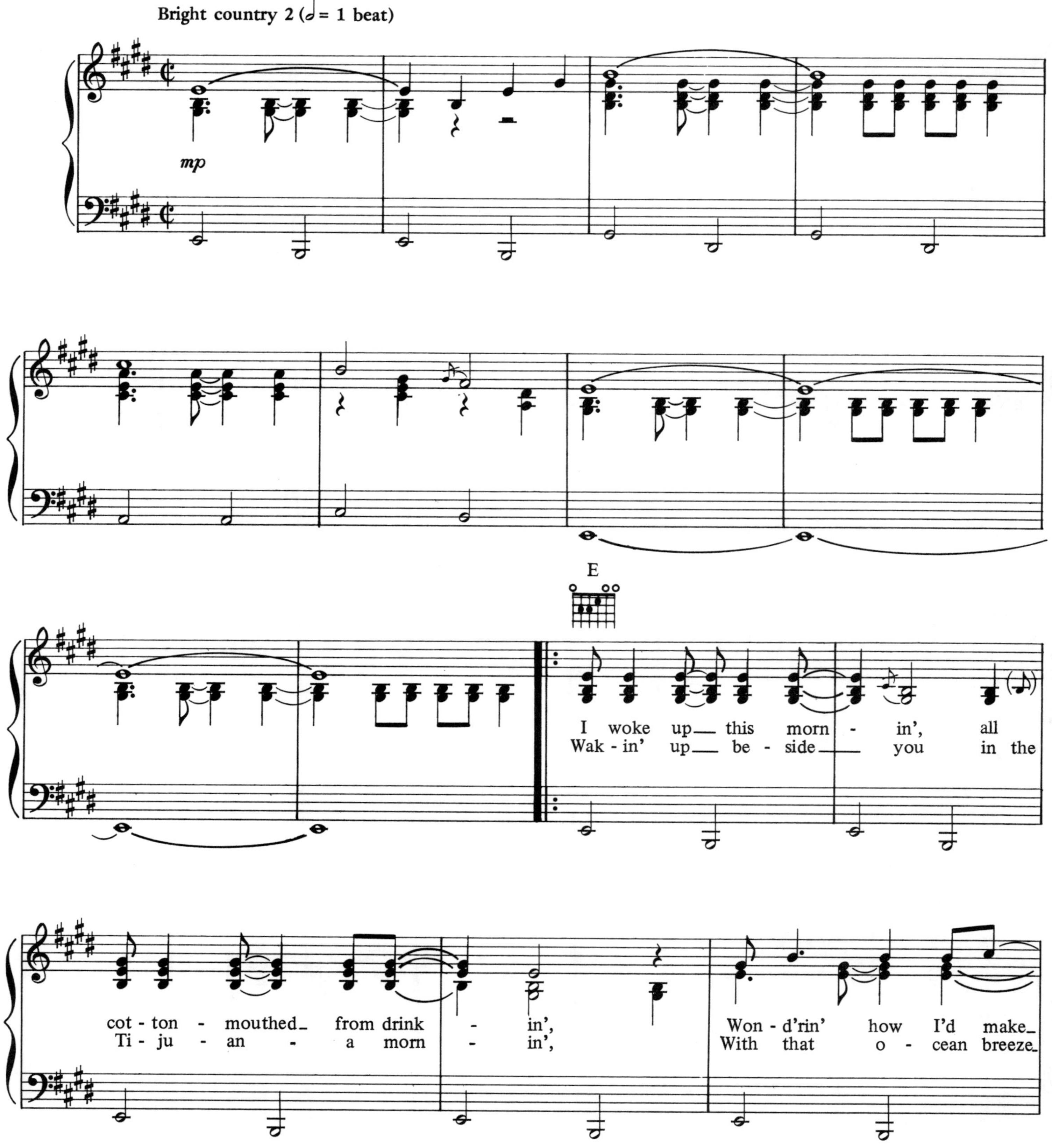

A
it through the day.
to keep us cool.
E
Wild - eyed and cra - zy,
Three weeks of lov - in,'
all burnt out from think-
twenty one nights of heav-
- in',
- en, I
won - d'rin' how the hell I's gon - na say:
stayed just long e - nough to be your fool.
A
Good -
Oh, good -

E
G♯m
4fr.
bye, Ma - rie, Oh, good - bye, Ma-rie,
A
Out the win - dow there's a lone - some high - way
C♯m
4fr.
B7
E
call - in' me. It was fun, Ma - rie,
G♯m
4fr.
but I got - ta run, Ma - rie; If I can -

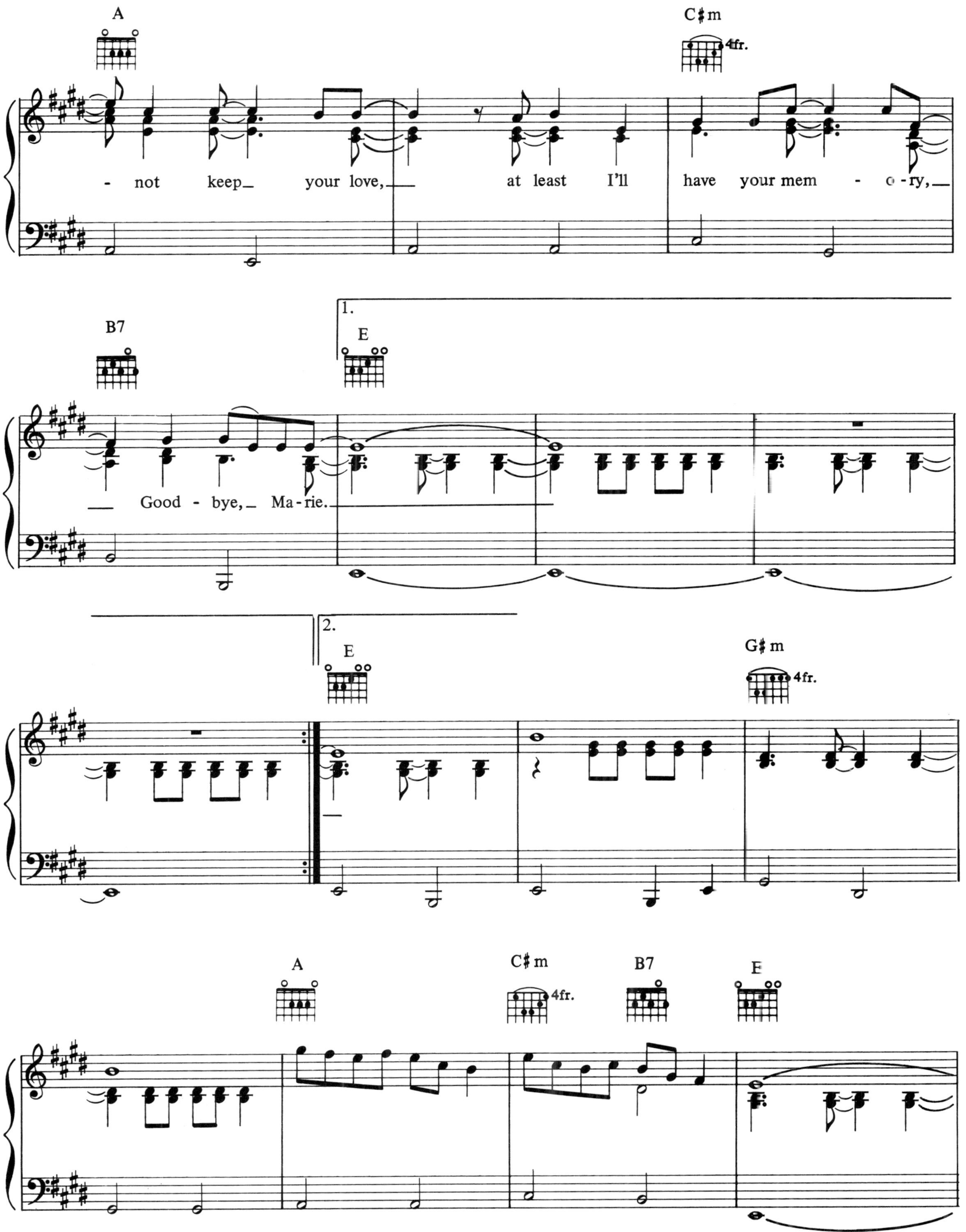
A
C♯m
4fr.
- not keep your love, at least I'll have your mem - o - ry,
B7
1.
E
Good - bye, Ma - rie.
2.
E
G♯m
4fr.
A
C♯m
4fr.
B7
E

E
Por fa - vor pour me
one more te - qui - la, I need all the cour - age I can find.
A
E
This time to - mor - row I'll be back in Hous - ton,
A
D.S. and fade
think - in' a - bout the girl I left be - hind.
So good -

I Want To Make You Smile

Words and Music by
Bill Medley

D/A
E7/A
A
D/A
E
E♭/B♭
F7/B♭
B♭
E♭/B♭
F
Each day goes by much too fast
A
D/A
E7/A
A
D/A
A
B♭
E♭/B♭
F7/B♭
B♭
E♭/B♭
B♭
To - mor - row soon be - comes the past.
E
F♯m
E/G♯
A
D/A
A
F
Gm
F/A
B♭
E♭/B♭
B♭
5fr.
3
Lost in the strug - gle of mak - in' my way,
E
F♯m
E/G♯
A
B/A
F
Gm
F/A
B♭
C/B♭
5fr.
Not tak - in' time e - nough to sim - ply say, "I love you; For -

E7 A B/A
F7 B♭ C/B♭
give me,_ I know it's been a while. I love you;
E E7 F A/E
F F7 G♭ B♭/F
I wan-na stop the world and make you smile."
E7sus4 E7 A D/A
F7sus4 F7 B♭ E♭/B♭
Too man-y days_
E7/A A D/A E A D/A
F7/B♭ B♭ E♭/B♭ F B♭ E♭/B♭
I for-get to take the time To say I love you and

E7/A
F7/Bb
A
Bb
D/A
Eb/Bb
A
Bb
E
F
F♯m
Gm
E/G♯
F/A
5fr.
thank you for be - ing mine.
Those sim - ple words I sometimes for -
- get to say
Will be on my lips on the wake of
each new day:
"I
B/A
C/Bb
love you;
For -
E7
F7
- give me
I know it's been a
while.
But you know I

B/A
C/B♭
E
F
E7
F7
love you, ___
I wan - na stop the world and make you
F
G♭
(falsetto)
A/E
B♭/F
smile, ___
If it's not too
Slower
E7sus4
F7sus4
E7
F7
N.C
late to make you
A
B♭
D/A
E♭/B♭
E7/A
F7/B♭
G9
A♭9
A
B♭
smile." ___

Tulsa Turnaround

Words and Music by
Alex Harvey and Larry Collins

G
A7
E7
O - ma - ha sher - iff and his boys get - tin' rea - dy to slaugh - ter They're
wish I was back in Ma - con tak - in' it eas - y, But if a
D
A
E7
look - in' for the man who turned on the may - or's daugh - ter.
man's gon - na eat fried chick - en he's got - ta get greas - y.
con 8
A7
N.C.
O - ma - ha hon - ey had a hold on a hell of a thing,
D
B7
Down in the hol - ler ev - 'ry eve - nin' you could hear her sing.

E
A
She say funk - y butt, showed me the Tul - sa Turn - a - round,
D
To Coda
B7
N.C.
stepped on my toes turned me on and turned me down, Fit me like a hand in a glove and taught me how to
1.
(N.C.)
love y'all.
E

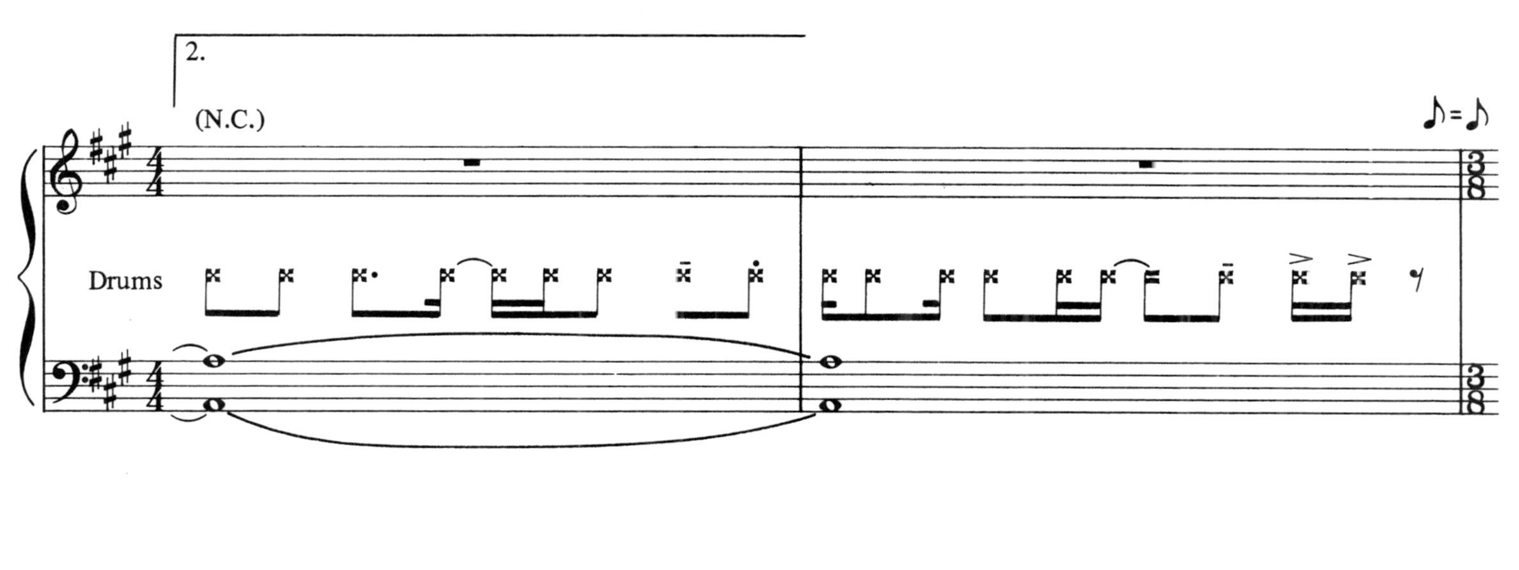
2.
(N.C.)
Drums

f

D.S. al Coda

Coda
B7
N.C.
A
Fit me like a hand in a glove__ and taught me how to love y'all.__
Slower
(In tempo)

Santiago Midnight Moonlight

Words and Music by
John Porter McMeans

Brightly, with a reggae feel

Guitar → D
(Capo up 3 frets)
Piano → F *

Señ - o - ri - ta, don't get me wrong, I'm a lone -

C D/G C/G G
E♭ F/B♭ E♭/B♭ B♭

ly boy, long, long way from home. An - oth - er fu - gi - tive of

* Guitarists: Chords are played finger style.

F♯m7-5
Am7-5
B7
D7
Em7
Gm7
A/B
C/D
Em7
Gm7
heart - break, I left it back in the States, so I'm here all a - lone.
Cmaj7
E♭maj7
C♯m7-5
Em7-5
This is cer - tain - ly a love - ly town, I was hop - in' you could
D
F
G
B♭
Am7
Cm7
show me a - round, Hop - in' may - be we could spend some time.
G/C
B♭/E♭
D
F
D/G
F/B♭
C/D
E♭/F
G
B♭
May - be you can get her off my mind. Spend some time in that San -

Am7 G/C D D/G G Am7 G/C D
Cm7 B♭/E♭ F F/B♭ B♭ Cm7 B♭/E♭ F
- ti - a - go mid - night moon - light, Trop - i - cal stars a -
Em7 Am7 G/C D D/G Em7
Gm7 Cm7 B♭/E♭ F F/B♭ Gm7
bove, San - ti - a - go mid - night moon - light, the
Am7 G/C D G
Cm7 B♭/E♭ F B♭ N.C.
To Coda
per - fect place to fall in love. I can't seem to get her
Now my days are turn - in' (To Coda)
D C D/G C/G G
F E♭ F/B♭ E♭/B♭ B♭
off of my mind, she was the one of a kind I was so luck - y to find.
* Instrumental omitted

F♯m7-5
Am7-5
B7
D7
We had e - ven talked of set - tl - ing down_ in some re - spect - ed sub - ur - ban A - mer -
Em7
Gm7
A/B
C/D
Em7
Gm7
Cmaj7
E♭maj7
- i - can town._ Did I tell you you have beau - ti - ful eyes_
C♯m7-5
Em7-5
D
F
G
B♭
as soft and dark as the trop - i - cal night?_ A mar - ga - ri - ta and a
Am7
Cm7
G/C
B♭/E♭
Dsus4
Fsus4
D/G
F/B♭
G
B♭
D.S. al Coda
mid - night smile,_ You made me want to stay a while And spend some time in your San-

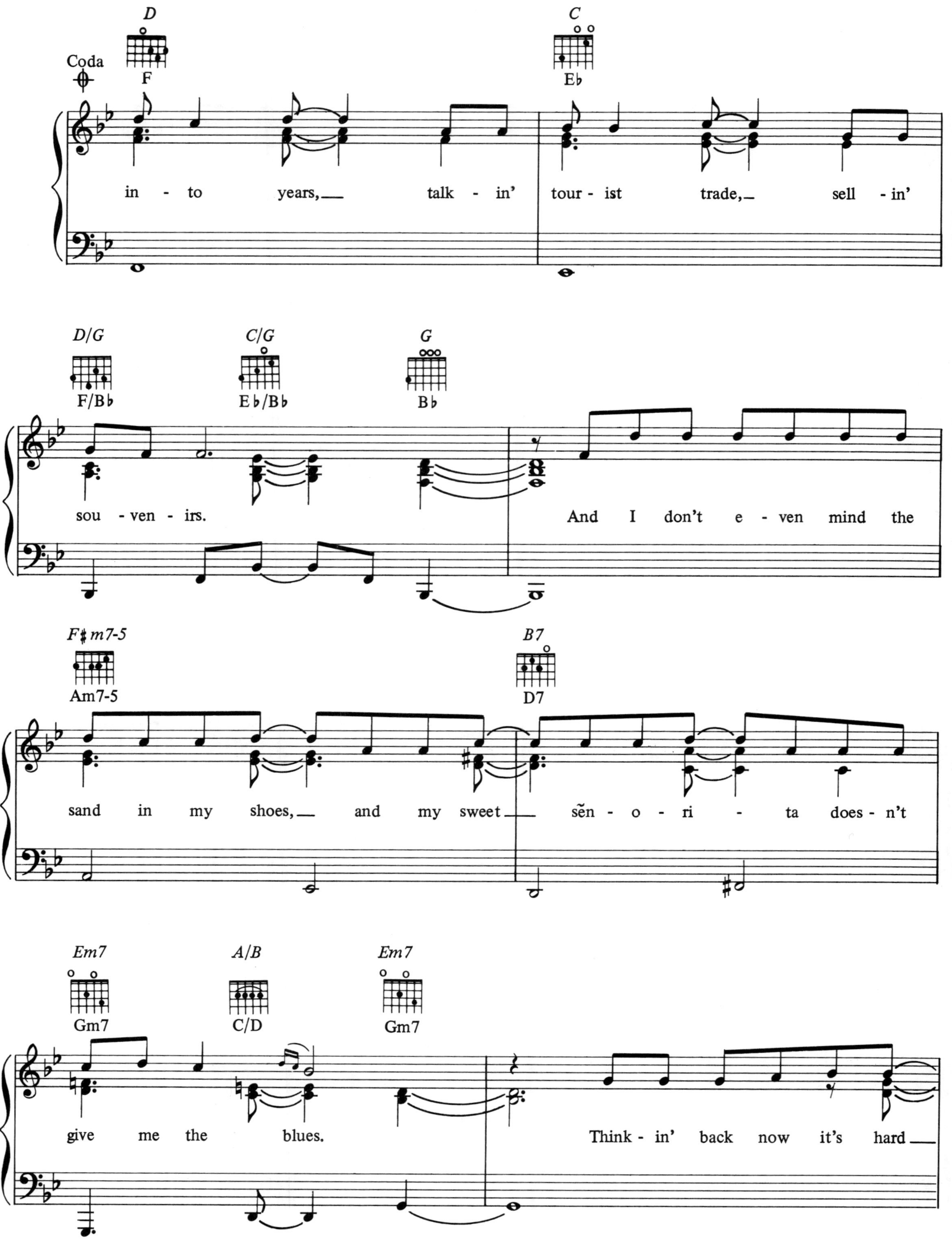
Coda
D
F
C
E♭
in - to years, talk - in' tour - ist trade, sell - in'
D/G
F/B♭
C/G
E♭/B♭
G
B♭
sou - ven - irs. And I don't e - ven mind the
F♯m7-5
Am7-5
B7
D7
sand in my shoes, and my sweet sẽn - o - ri - ta does - n't
Em7
Gm7
A/B
C/D
Em7
Gm7
give me the blues. Think - in' back now it's hard

Cmaj7
E♭maj7
C♯m7-5
Em7-5
to say
why I left the good ole
D
F
G
B♭
U. S. A.
As I re - call I left some
Am7
Cm7
G/C
B♭/E♭
D
F
girl back there, but I swear I can't e - ven re - mem-
D/G
F/B♭
C/D
E♭/F
G
B♭
- ber her name.
I'm just think - in' 'bout

Am7 G/C D D/G G
Cm7 B♭/E♭ F F/B♭ B♭
San - ti - a - go mid - night moon - light,
Am7 G/C D Em7 Am7 G/C D
Cm7 B♭/E♭ F Gm7 Cm7 B♭/E♭ F
Trop - i - cal stars a - bove, San - ti - a - go mid - night
D/G Em7 Am7 G/C D 1. G
F/B♭ Gm7 Cm7 B♭/E♭ F B♭
N.C.
moon - light, the per - fect place to fall in love.
2.
G/C D G/C D G
B♭/E♭ F B♭/E♭ F B♭
N.C.
N.C.
let's fall in, you can fall in love.

One Man's Woman

Words and Music by
Steve Glassmeyer

Em
Em/D
C
e - le - va - tor takes her to her lov - er, She
thinks a - bout her hus - band when it's o - ver, But she
Em
Em/D
C
thinks a - bout his wife at home a - sleep, And she
jus - ti - fies her love af - fair some - how. And she
Em
Em/D
C
knows it must be pain - ful to dis - cov - er That the
knows it can't go on like this for - ev - er, But she
C/D
C
G
man you love's not al - ways yours to keep.
takes it all from day to day for now.
Well, she's

1.
C
G/D
D7
one man's ___ wom - an and
one man's cn the side.___
G
C/G
She
2.
C
D/C
C
G
one man's ___ wom - an and
one man's on the side; ___ She
C
G/B
A7
D
won - ders why it takes ___ two men to
keep her sat - is - fied
Well, she's a

Chorus
C
D/C
C
G
one man's bride and she's one man's on the side; She
C
G/B
A7
D
won - ders why it takes two men to keep her sat - is - fied. Well, she's a
C
G/B
B7
Em
Em/D
hard - work - ing house - wife and right now she's oc - cu - pied. Well, she's
C
G/D
D7
G
one man's wom - an and one man's on the side. Yes, she's

C
G/B
B7
Em
Em/D
hard - work - ing house - wife and right now she's oc - cu - pied. Well, she's
(but)
C
G/D
D7
G
one man's wom - an and one man's on the side. Yes, she's
C
G/D
D7
G
C
one man's wom - an and one man's on the side.
D
G
C/G
G
Slower

In And Out Of Your Heart

Words and Music by Randy Cullers,
Thomas Cain, Alan Rush and Dennis Linde

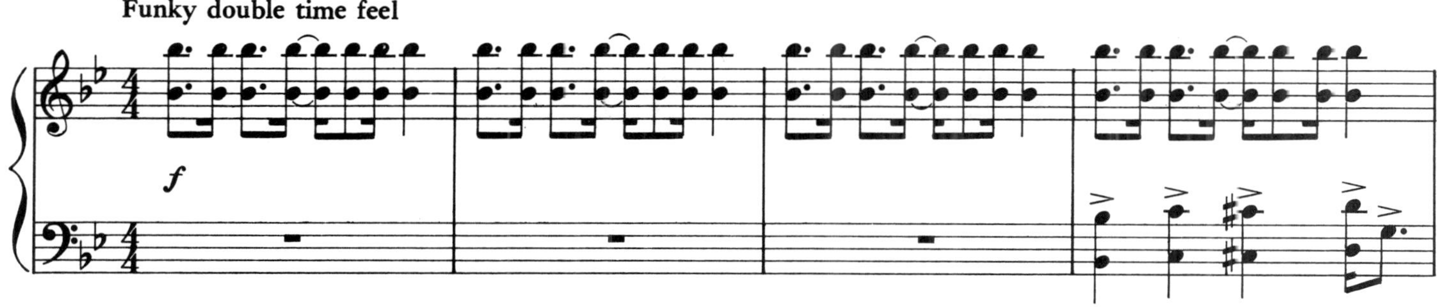

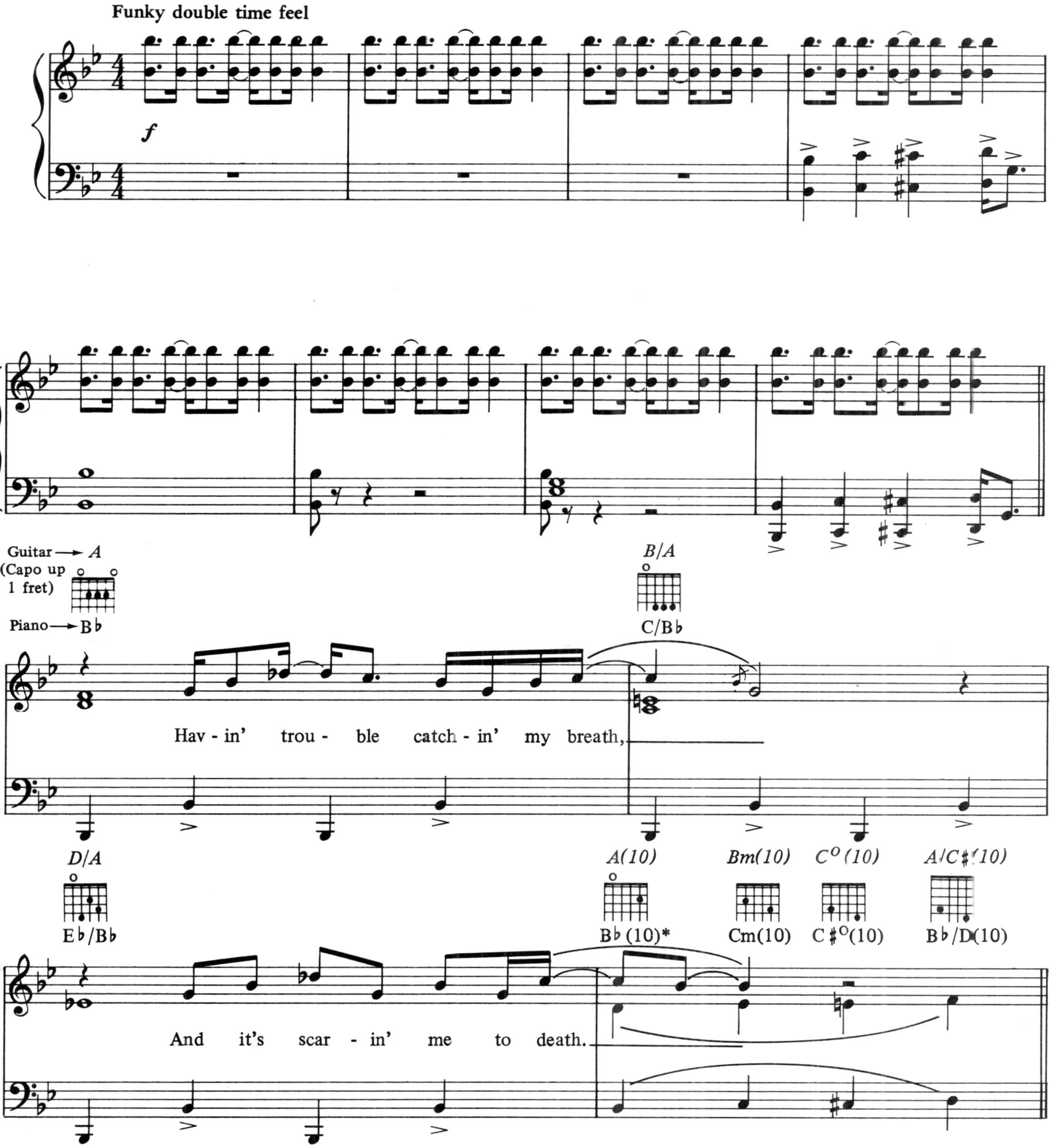
Funky double time feel
f
Guitar → A
(Capo up 1 fret)
Piano → B♭
B/A
C/B♭
Hav - in' trou - ble catch - in' my breath,
D/A
E♭/B♭
A(10)
B♭(10)*
Bm(10)
Cm(10)
C°(10)
C♯°(10)
A/C♯(10)
B♭/D(10)
And it's scar - in' me to death.

*(10) means play open 10th only, not the full chord.

A
B♭
B/A
C/B♭
1. Doc - tor, take a look at me,
2. Instrumental
D/A
E♭/B♭
A(10)
B♭(10)
Bm(10)
Cm(10)
C°(10)
C♯°(10)
A/C♯(10)
B♭/D(10)
Tell the truth, what do you see?
A
B♭
B/A
C/B♭
Is it some - thing you can cure?
Doc - tor, can you find a cure?
D/A
E♭/B♭
A(10)
B♭(10)
Bm(10)
Cm(10)
C°(10)
C♯°(10)
A/C♯(10)
B♭/D(10)
Tell me are you real - ly sure?

A
B♭
B/A
C/B♭
He said, "Take a look at your chart;
D/A
E♭/B♭
A(10) Bm(10) C°(10) A/C♯(10)
B♭(10) Cm(10) C♯°(10) B♭/D(10)
Some - thing's mov - in' in and out - ta your heart.
Dmaj7
7fr.
E♭maj7
C♯m7
5fr.
Dm7
Blood pres - sure's go - in' up,
Dmaj7
7fr.
E♭maj7
C♯m7
5fr.
Dm7
Temp - 'ra - ture is on the rise,

Cmaj7
5fr.
D♭maj7
Bm7
Cm7
All the symp - toms point to love,
B♭maj7
C♭maj7
Am
B♭m
E+
F+
To Coda
You need her treat - ment to sur - vive.
long gliss
A
B♭
B/A
C/B♭
D/A
E♭/B♭
And it's been there from the start,
Mov - in' in and out - ta your
D.S. al Coda
Coda
A(10)
Bm(10)
C°(10)
A/C♯(10)
B♭(10)
Cm(10)
C♯°(10)
B♭/D(10)
A
B♭
B/A
C/B♭
heart."
Doc - tor, can you find a cure?

D/A
E♭/B♭
A(10) Bm(10) C°(10) A/C♯(10) A
B♭(10) Cm(10) C♯°(10) B♭/D(10) B♭
Tell me are you real - ly sure?
He said, "Take a look at your
B/A
C/B♭
D/A
E♭/B♭
N.C.
chart;
Some - thing's mov - in' in and out - ta your heart.
Repeat and fade
A
B♭
B/A
C/B♭
D/A
E♭/B♭
A(10) Bm(10) C°(10) A/C♯(10)
B♭(10) Cm(10) C♯°(10) B♭/D(10)
5

Coward of the County

Words and Music by
Roger Bowling and Billy Edd Wheeler

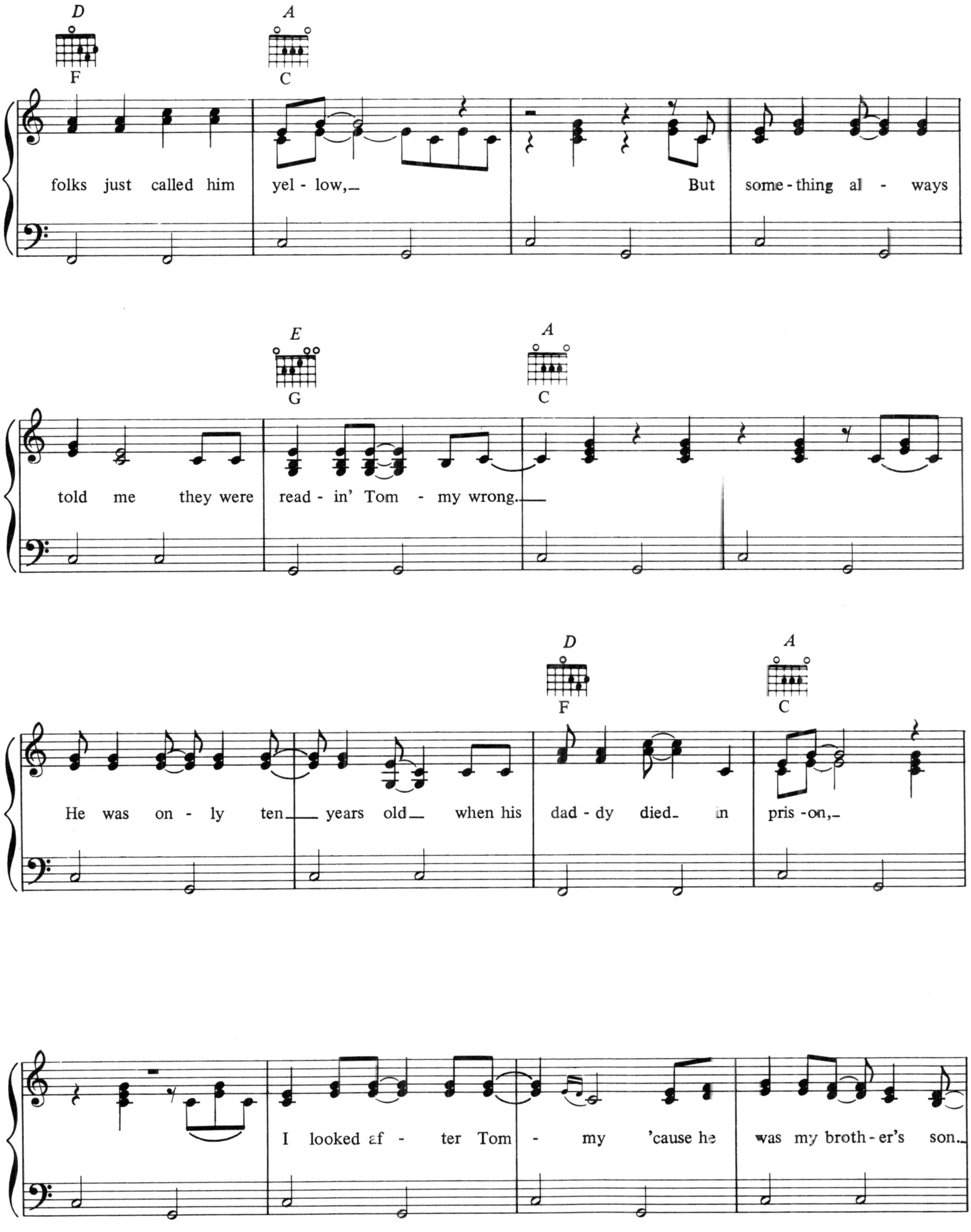

D A
F C
folks just called him yel - low, — But some - thing al - ways

E A
G C
told me they were read - in' Tom - my wrong. —

D A
F C
He was on - ly ten — years old — when his dad - dy died — in pris - on, —

E
G
A
C
I still re-call the final words my
D
F
A
C
broth-er said to Tom-my,
"Son, my life is o-
ver, but yours is just be-gun.
Chorus 1
A
C
Prom-ise me, son, not to do the things I've done,
D
F
A
C
done,

D
A
E
F
C
G
Walk a - way from trou - ble if you can.
A
D
A
C
F
C
It won't mean you're weak if you turn the oth - er cheek, I
D
E
F
G
hope you're old e - nough to un - der - stand: Son,
E7
A
G7
C (Guitarists: Slide capo to 4th fret)
you don't have to fight to be a man." There's

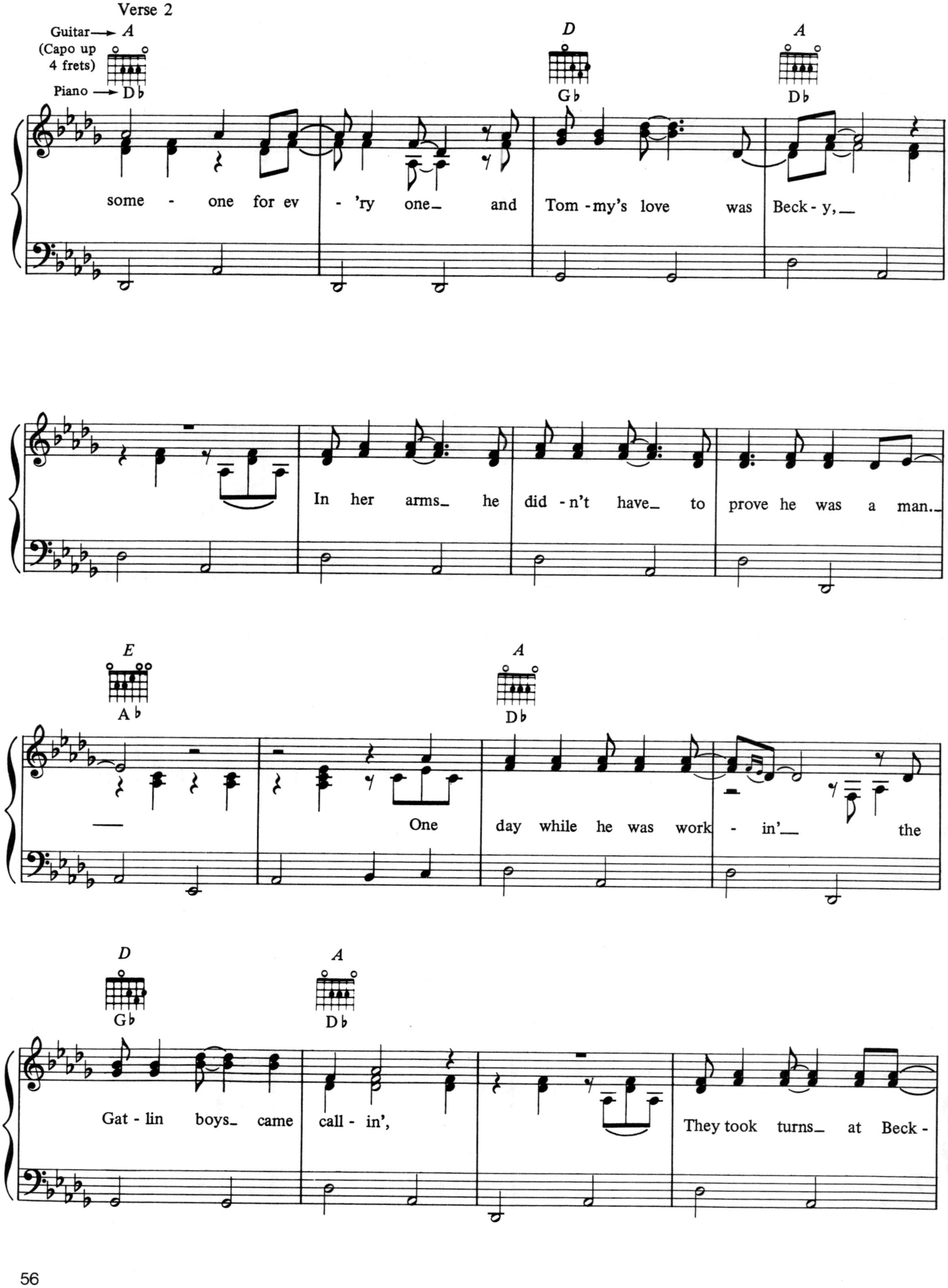

In her arms_ he did - n't have_ to prove he was a man._

E
A♭
A
D♭

One day while he was work - in'_ the

D
G♭
A
D♭

Gat - lin boys_ came call - in',

They took turns_ at Beck -

E
Ab
A
Db
-y,
(Spoken) there was
three of
them!
Tom-my o-pened up
D
Gb
A
Db
the door and
saw his Beck-y
cry-in',
The
E
Ab
torn dress, the
shat-tered look was
more than he could
stand.
A
Db
D
Gb
He
reached a-bove the fire
-place and took
down his dad-dy's

A
D♭
pic - ture. As his tears fell on his dad - dy's face, he
E
A♭
A
D♭
heard these words a - gain:
Chorus 2
A
D♭
D
G♭
A
D♭
"Prom - ise me, son, not to do the things I've done,
D
G♭
A
D♭
E
A♭
Walk a - way from trou - ble if you can.

A
Db
D
Gb
A
Db
It won't mean you're weak if you turn the oth - er cheek, I
A
Db
D
Gb
E
Ab
hope you're old e - nough to un - der - stand:
Son,
E7
Ab7
A
Db
(Guitarists: Slide capo to 5th fret)
you don't have to fight to be a man."
The
Verse 3
Guitar → A
(Capo up 5 frets)
Piano → D
D
G
A
D
Gat - lin boys just laughed at him when he walked in - to the bar - room.

One of them got up and met him half - way 'cross the floor.
E
A
A
D
When Tom - my turned a - round they said, "Hey
D
G
A
D
look! ol' yel - low's leav - in'."
But you coulda heard a
E
A
A
D
pin drop when Tommy stopped and blocked the door.

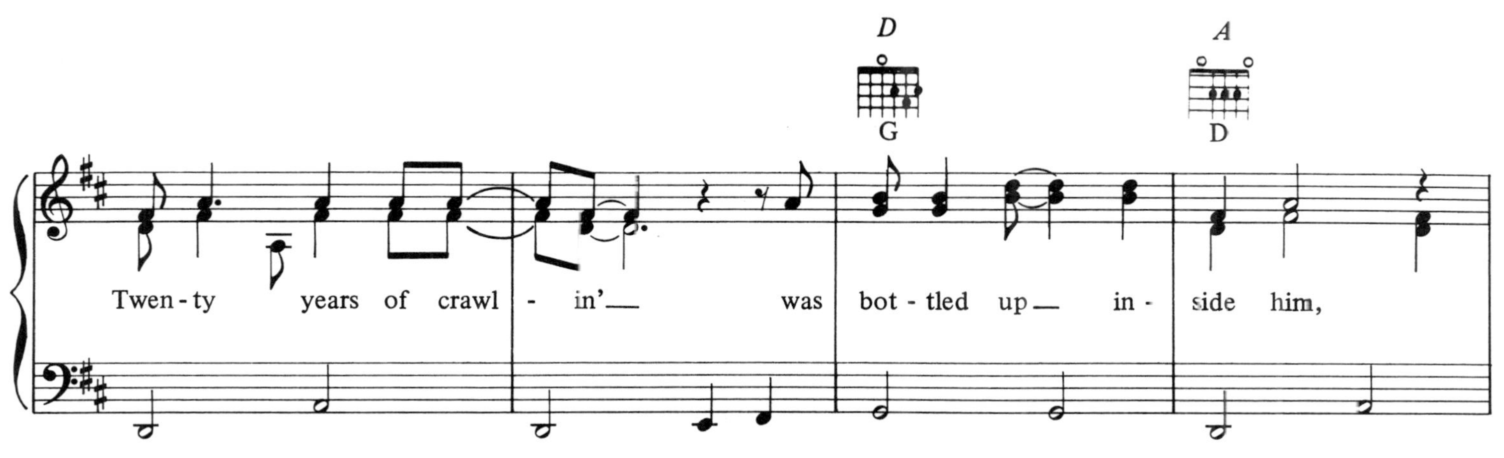
D
A
G
D
Twen-ty years of crawl - in'— was bot-tled up— in - side him,

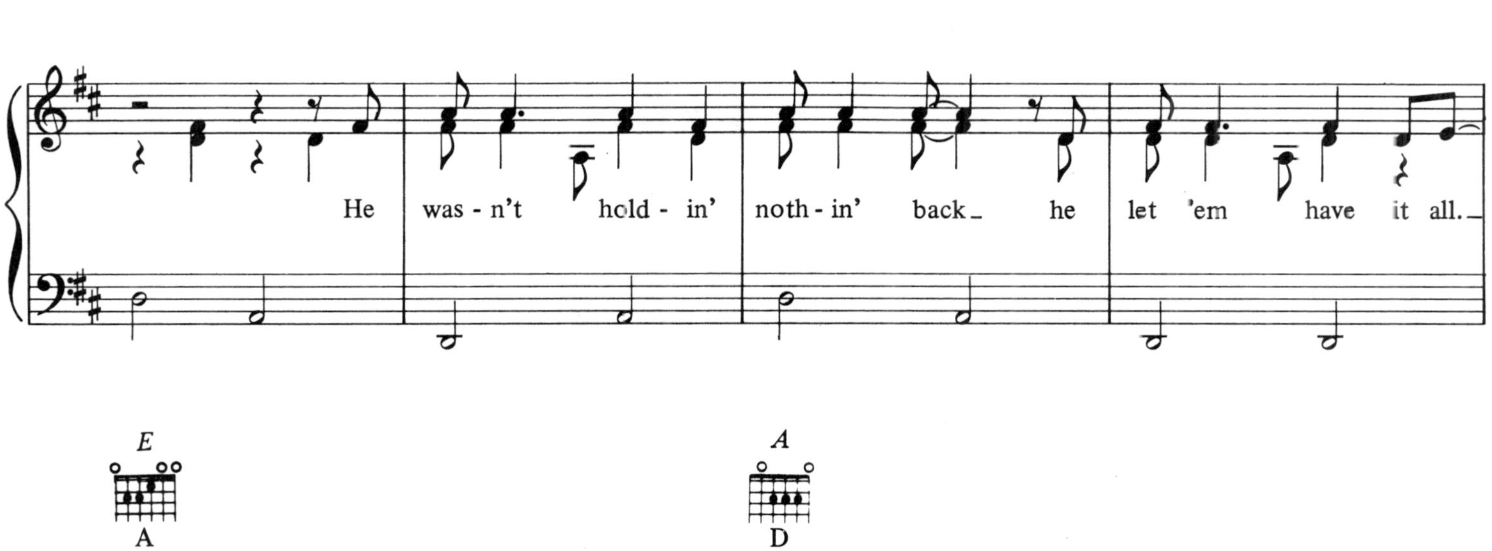
He was-n't hold-in' noth-in' back— he let 'em have it all.—

E
A
A
D
When Tom-my left— the bar - room not a

D
A
G
D
Gat-lin boy was stand-in', He said, "This one's— for Beck-

E
A
A
D
- y," As he watched the last one fall. And I heard him say, "I
Chorus 3
A
D
D
G
A
D
prom - ised you, Dad, not to do the things you done, I
D
G
A
D
E
A
walk a - way from trou - ble when I can. Now
A
D
D
G
A
D
please don't think I'm weak, I did - n't turn the oth - er cheek, And

D
E
G
A
Pop - pa, I sure hope you un - der - stand:
Some -
E7
A
A7
D
times you got - ta fight when you're a man."
A
D
Tag
Ev - 'ry - one con - sid - ered him the
D
G
N.C.
A
D
cow - ard of the coun - ty.
Slower